Fanciful Creatures

A Coloring Book for Adults

By Katu Matson

Featuring 17 original drawings and 2 bonus pages.

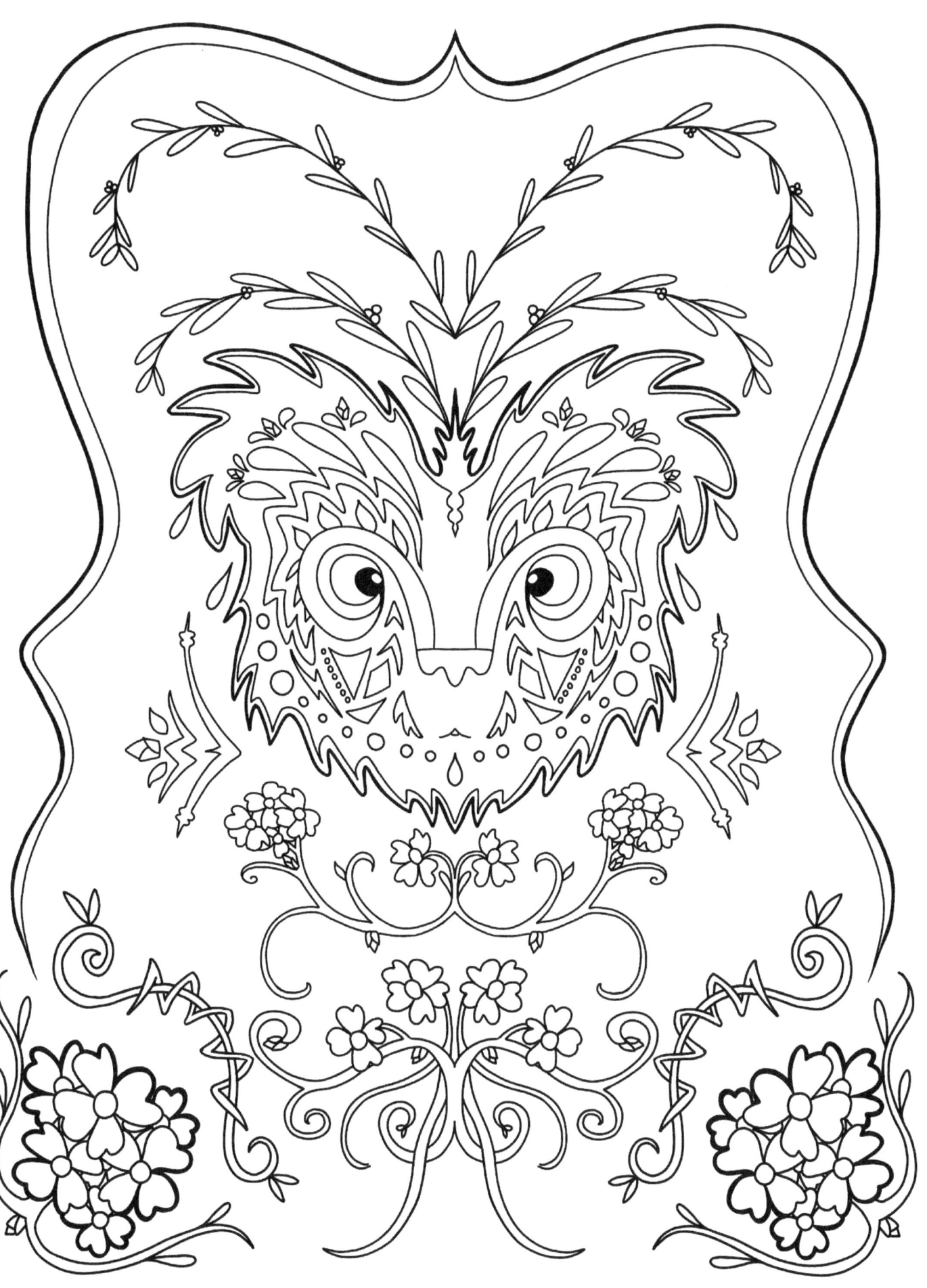

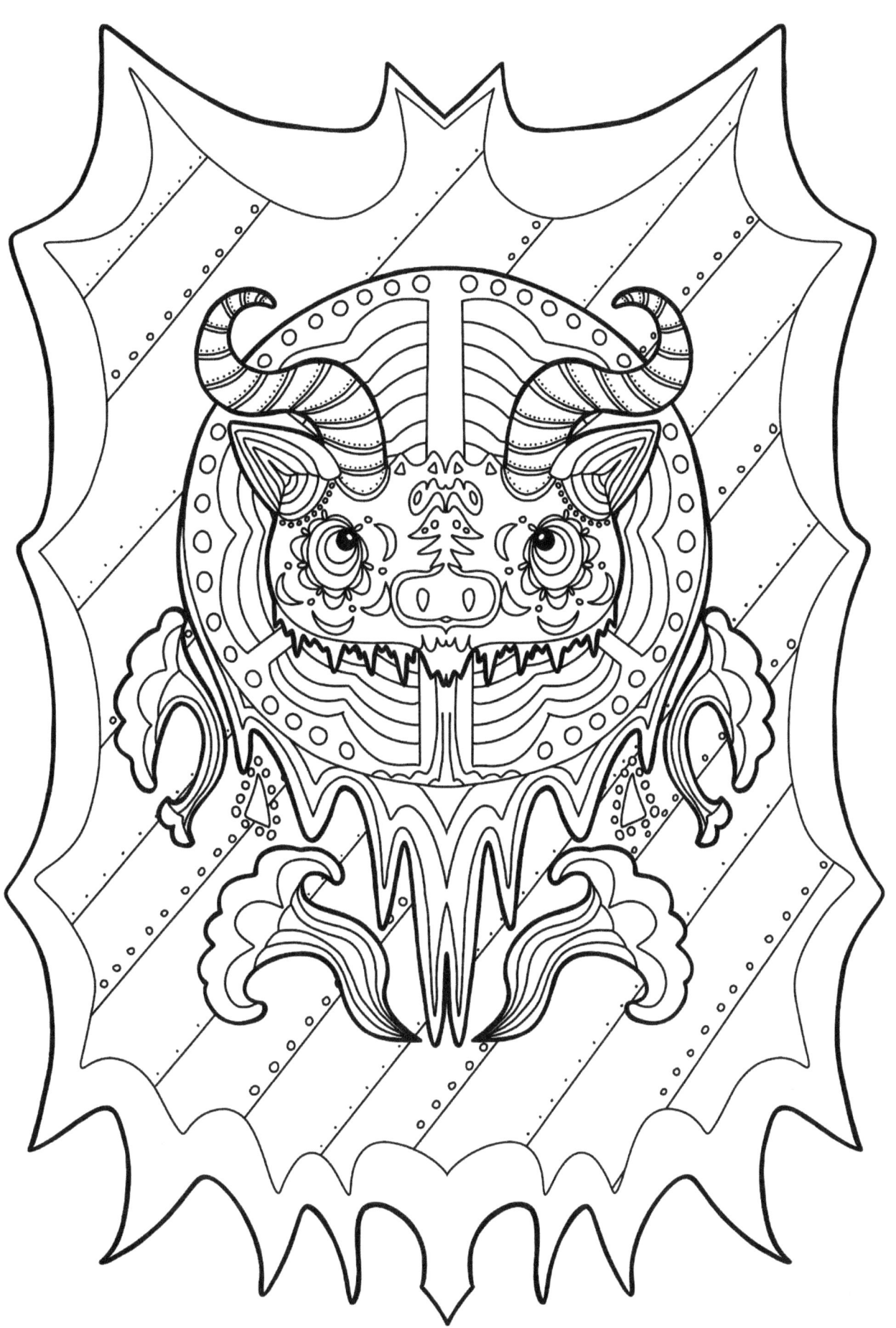

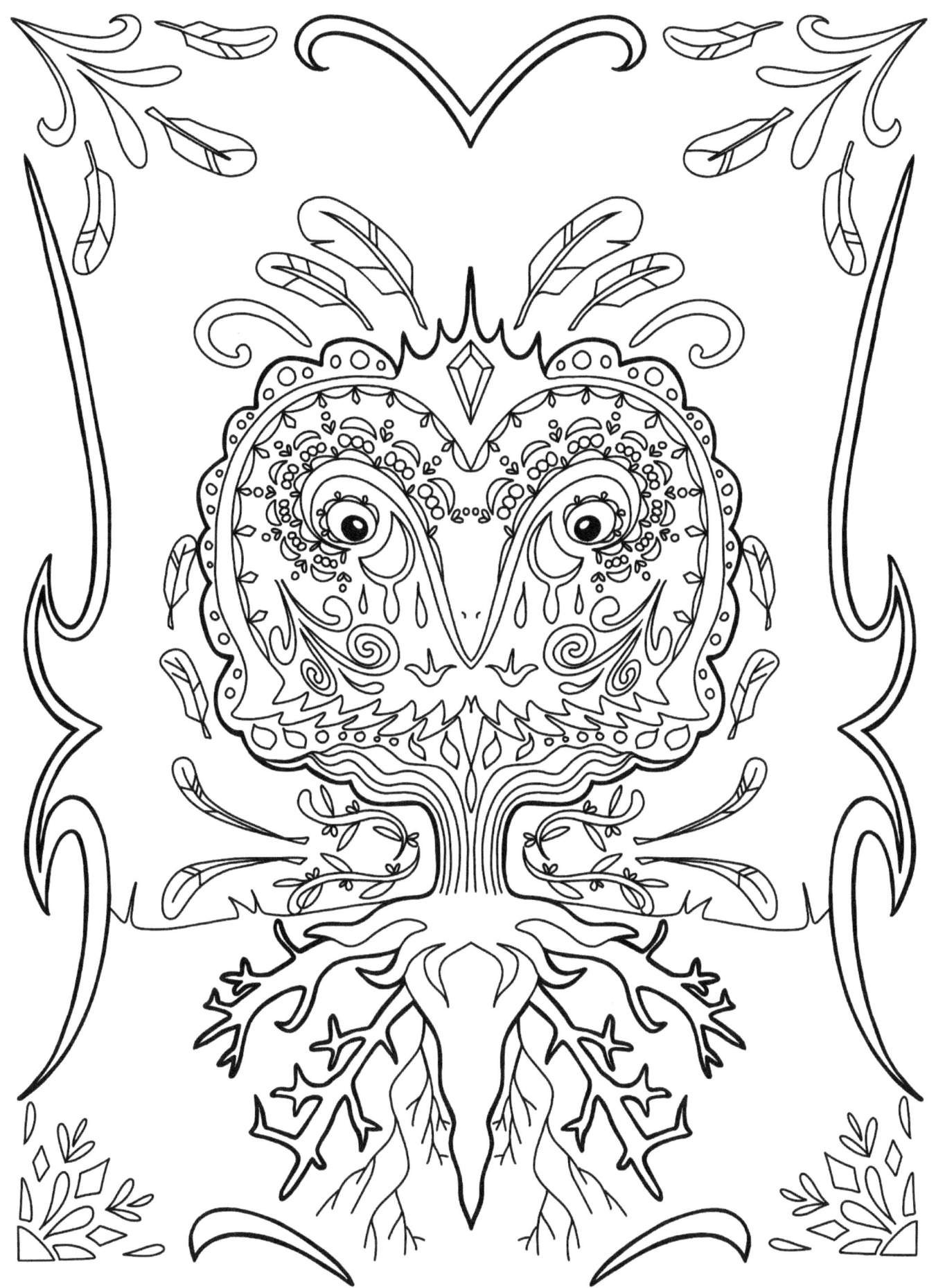

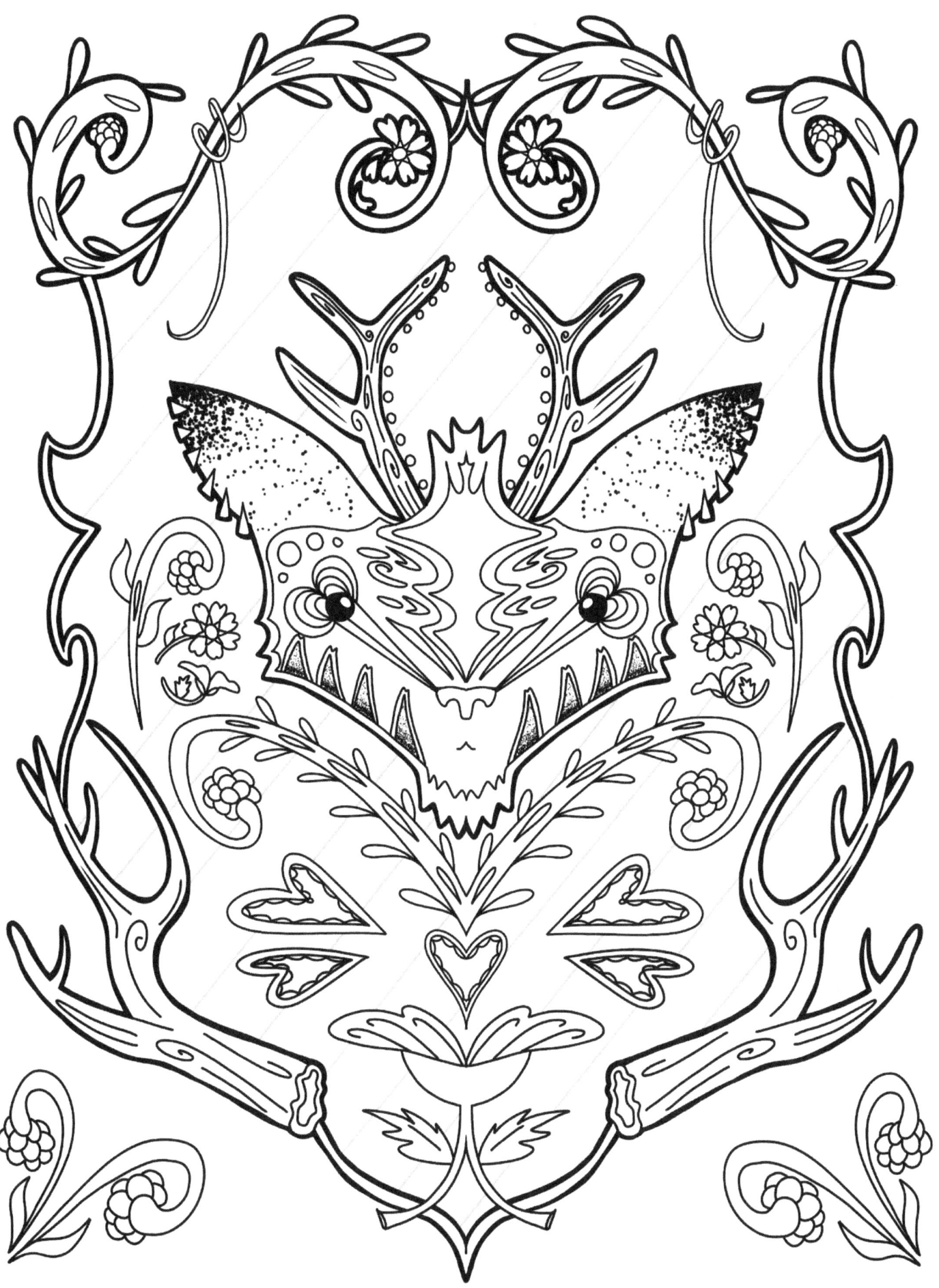

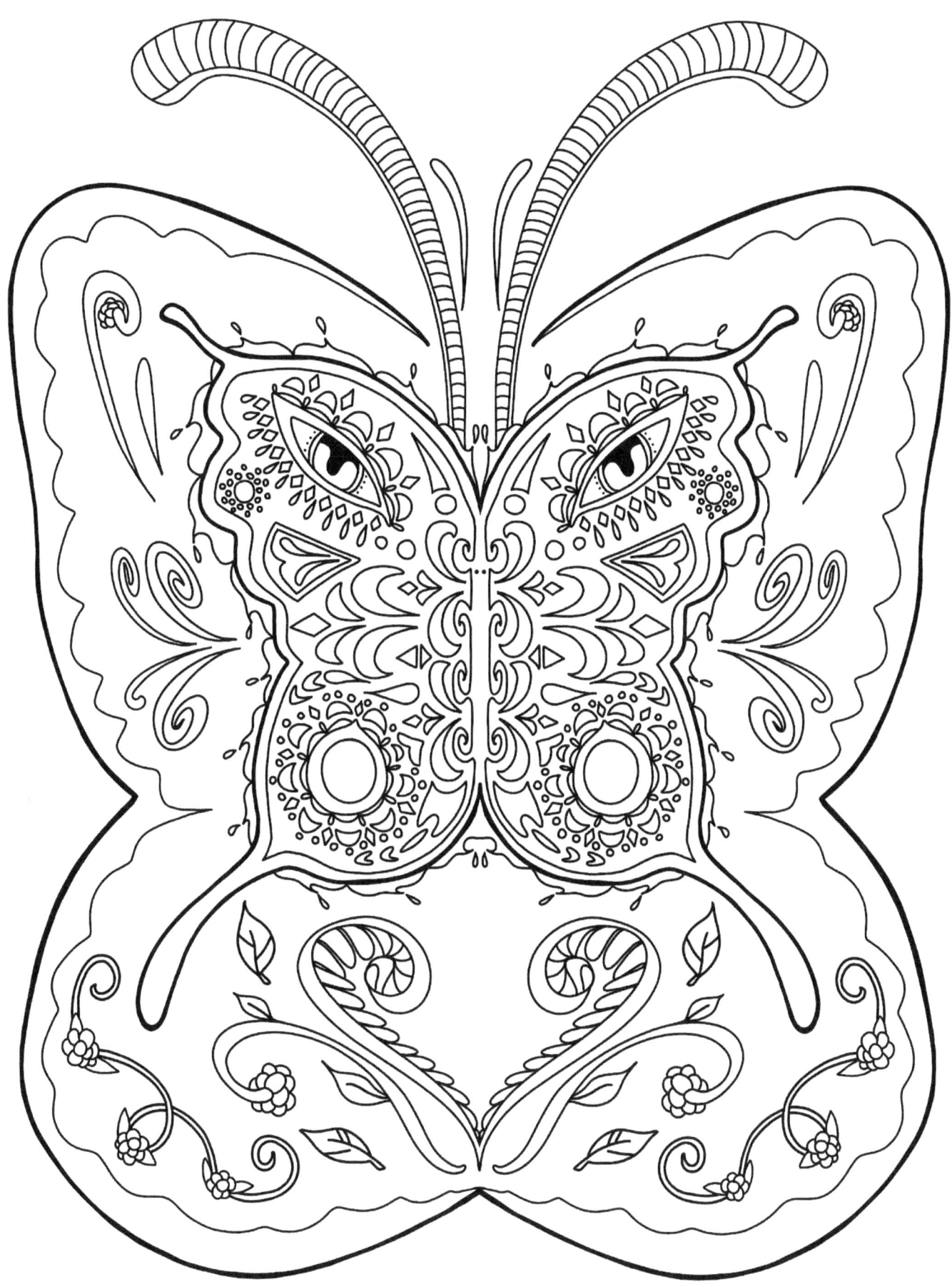

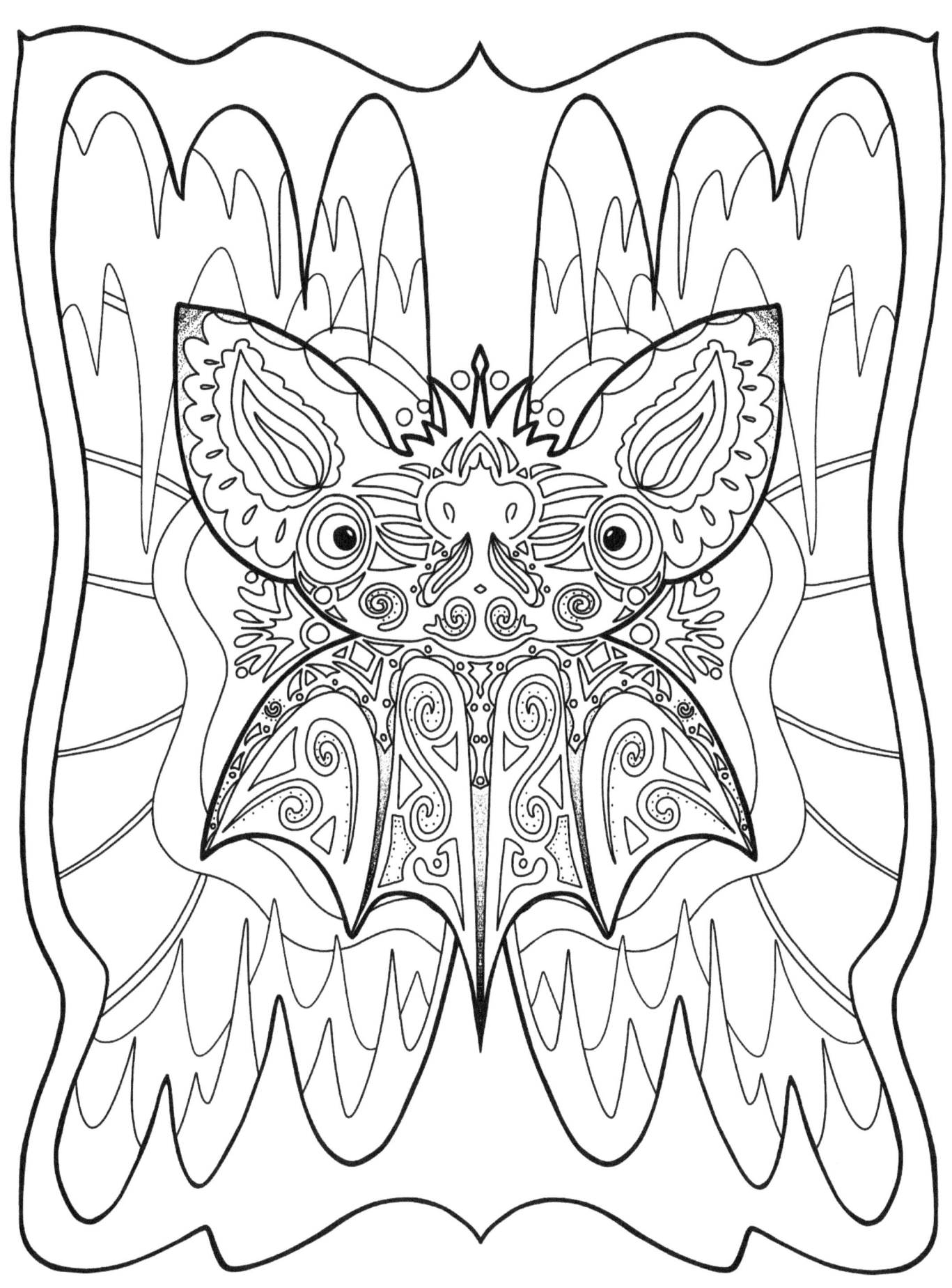

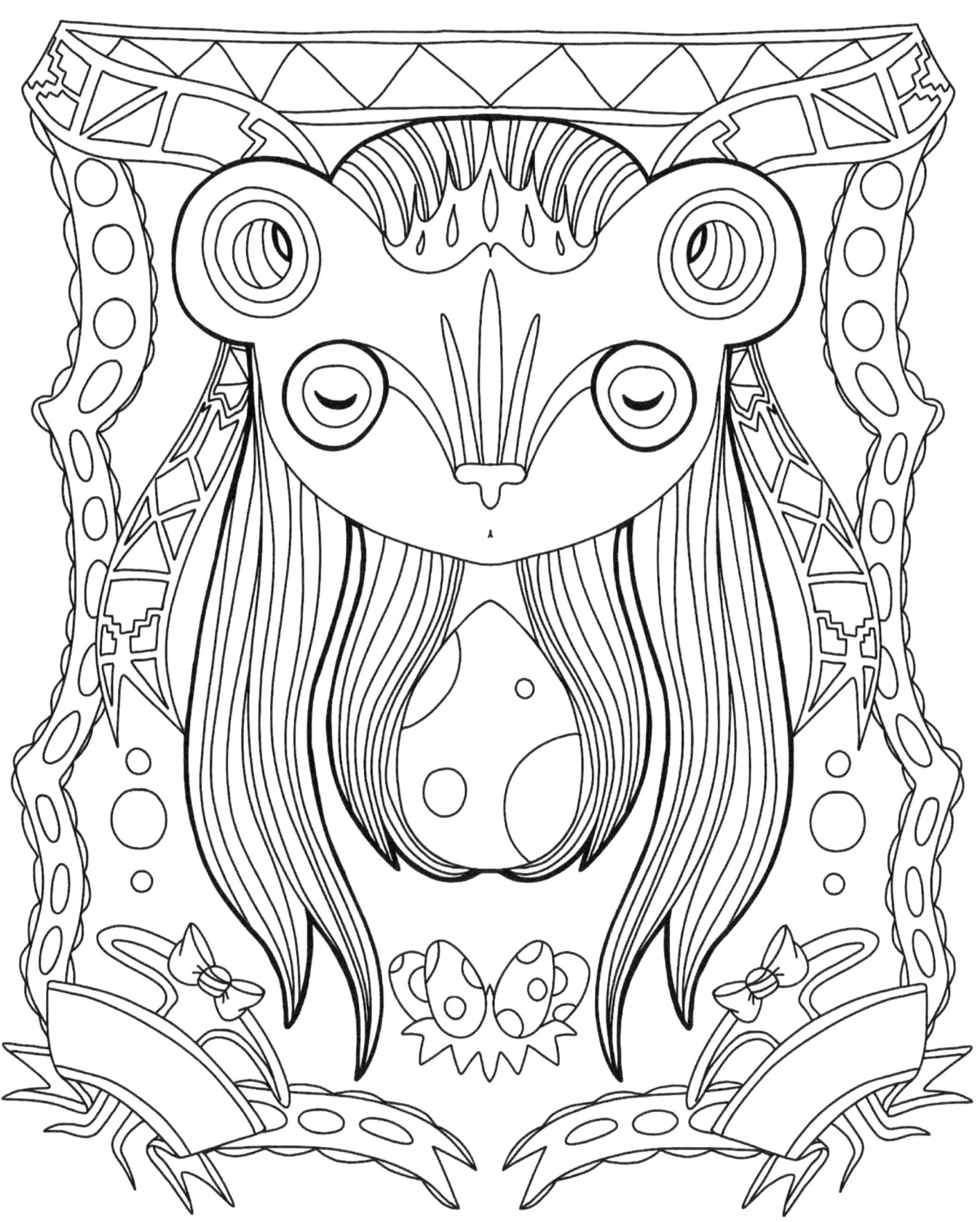

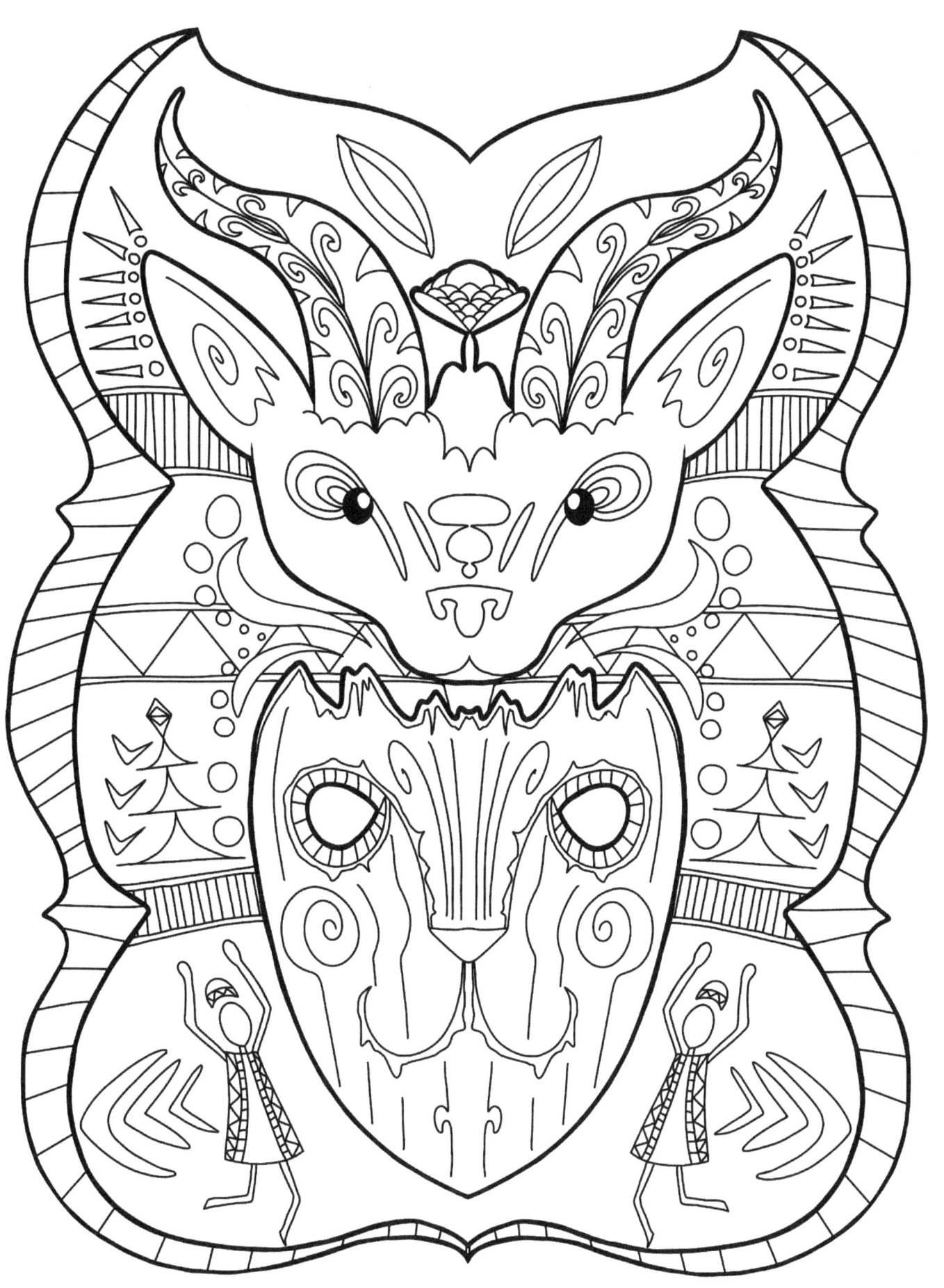

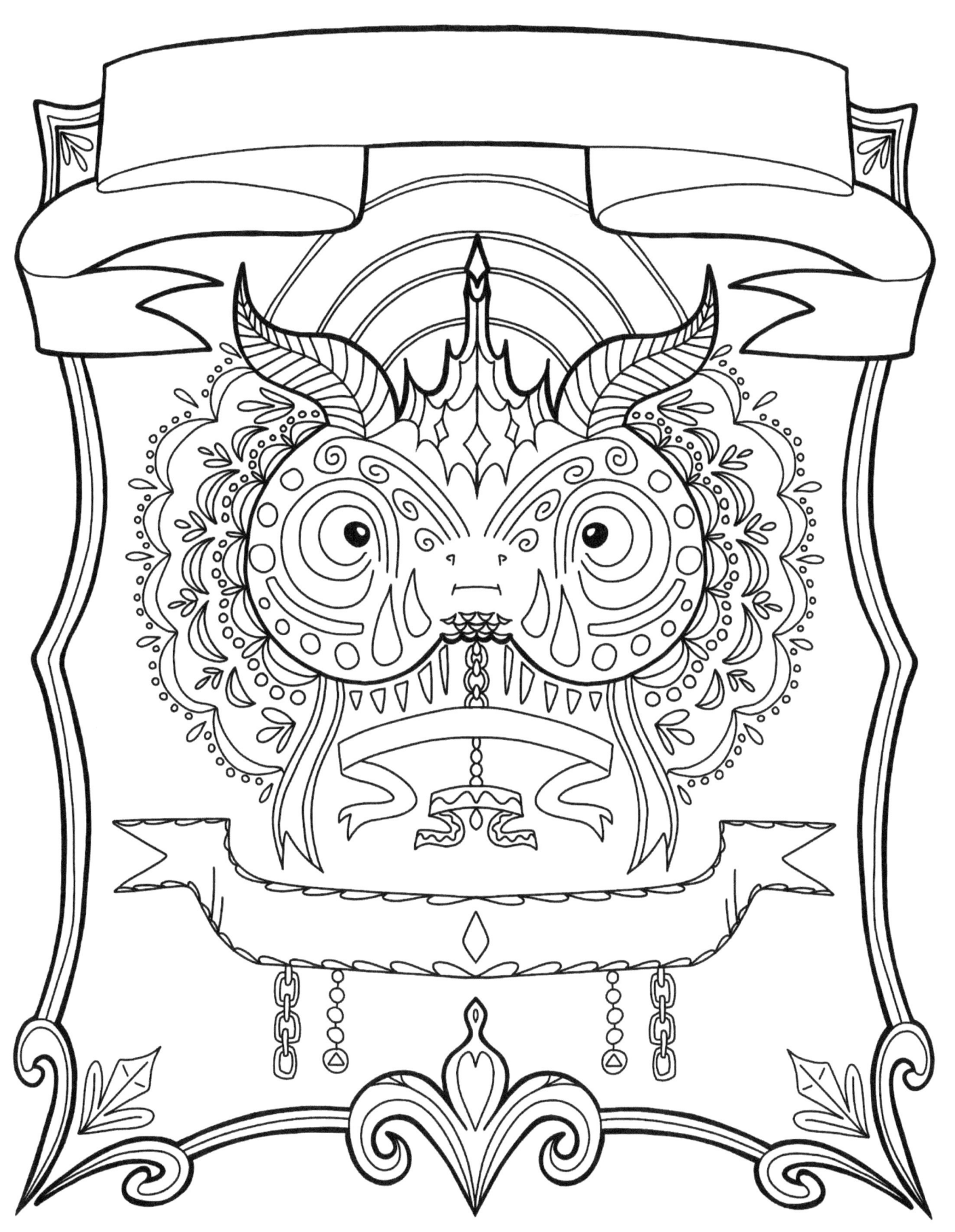

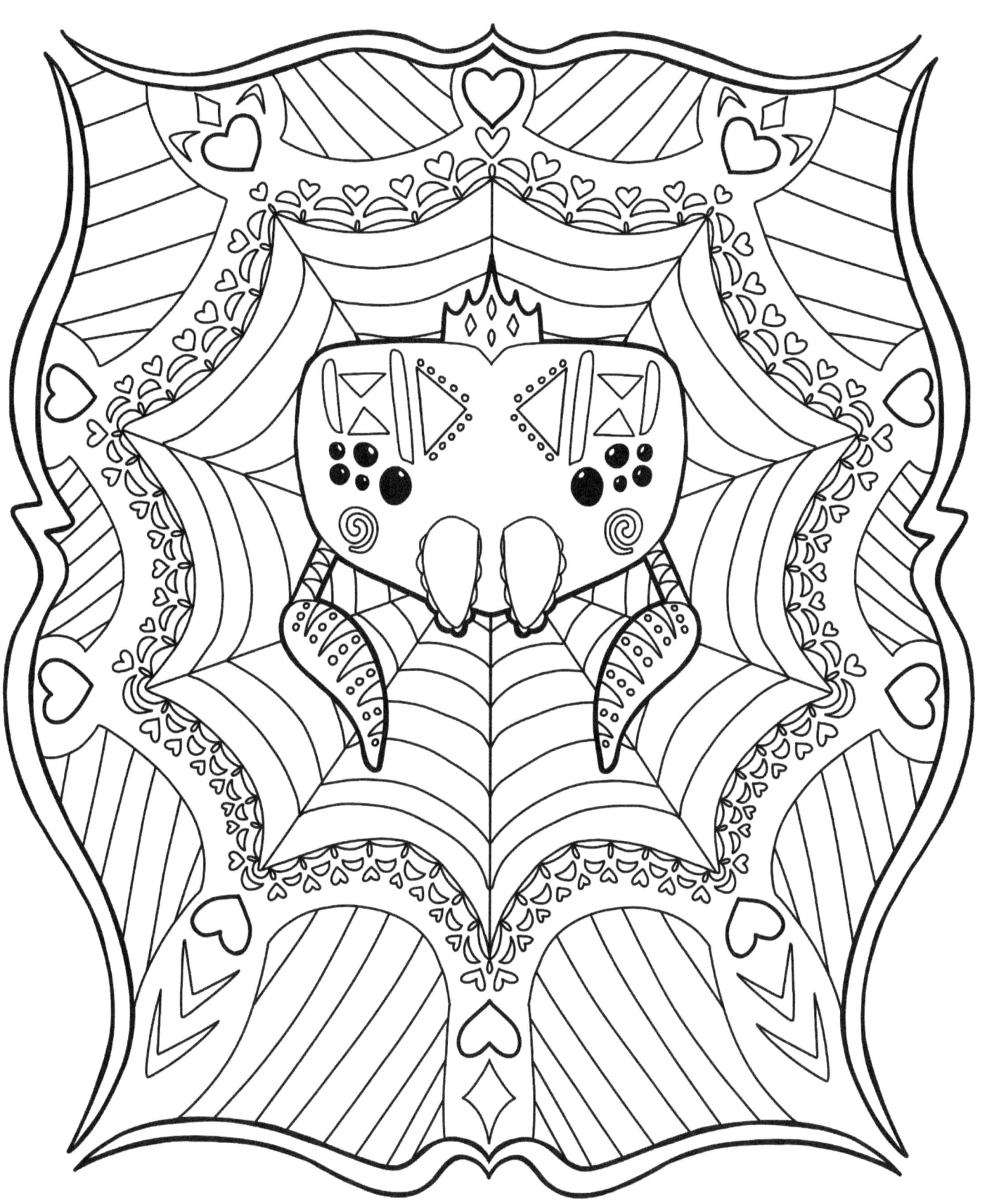

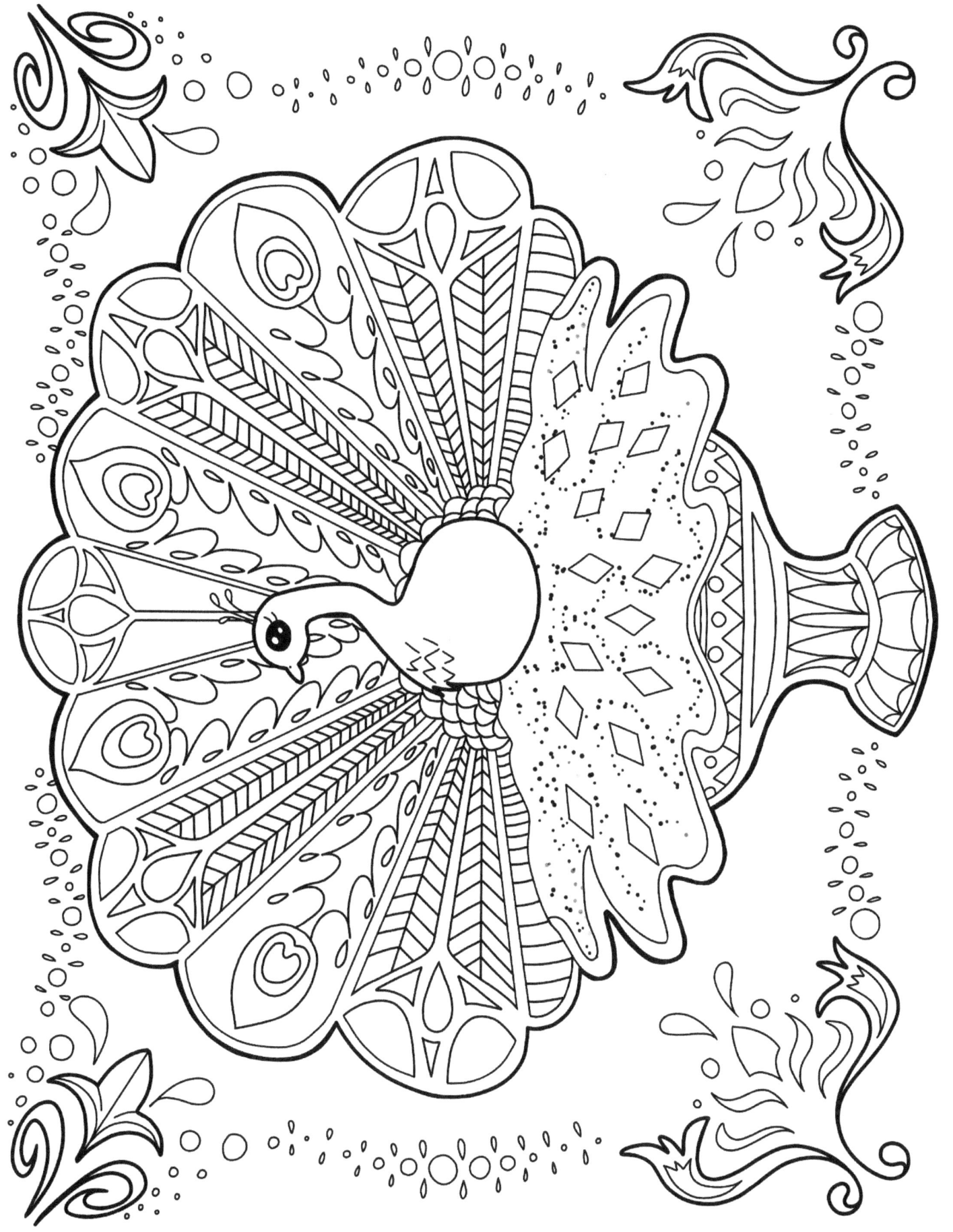

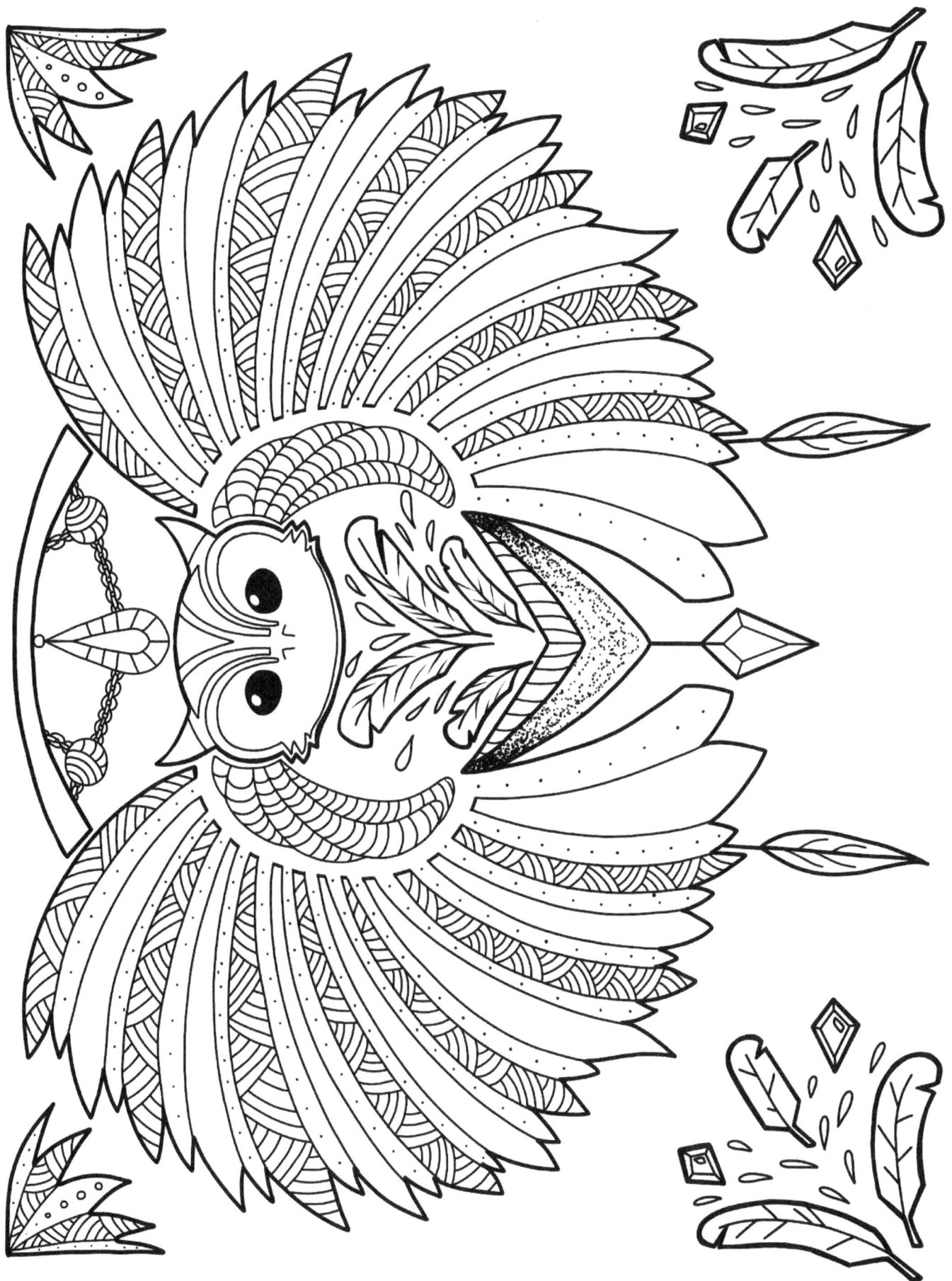

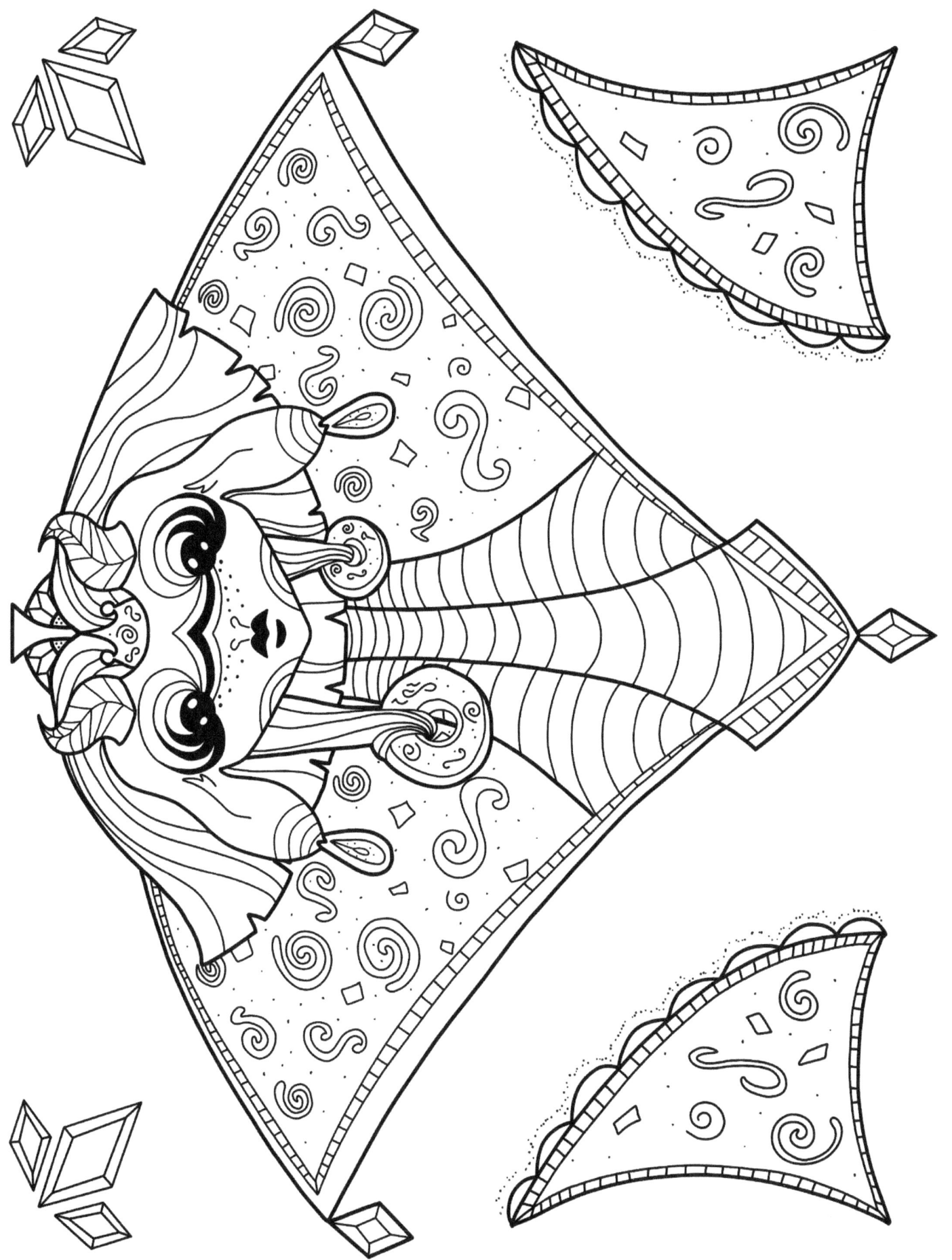

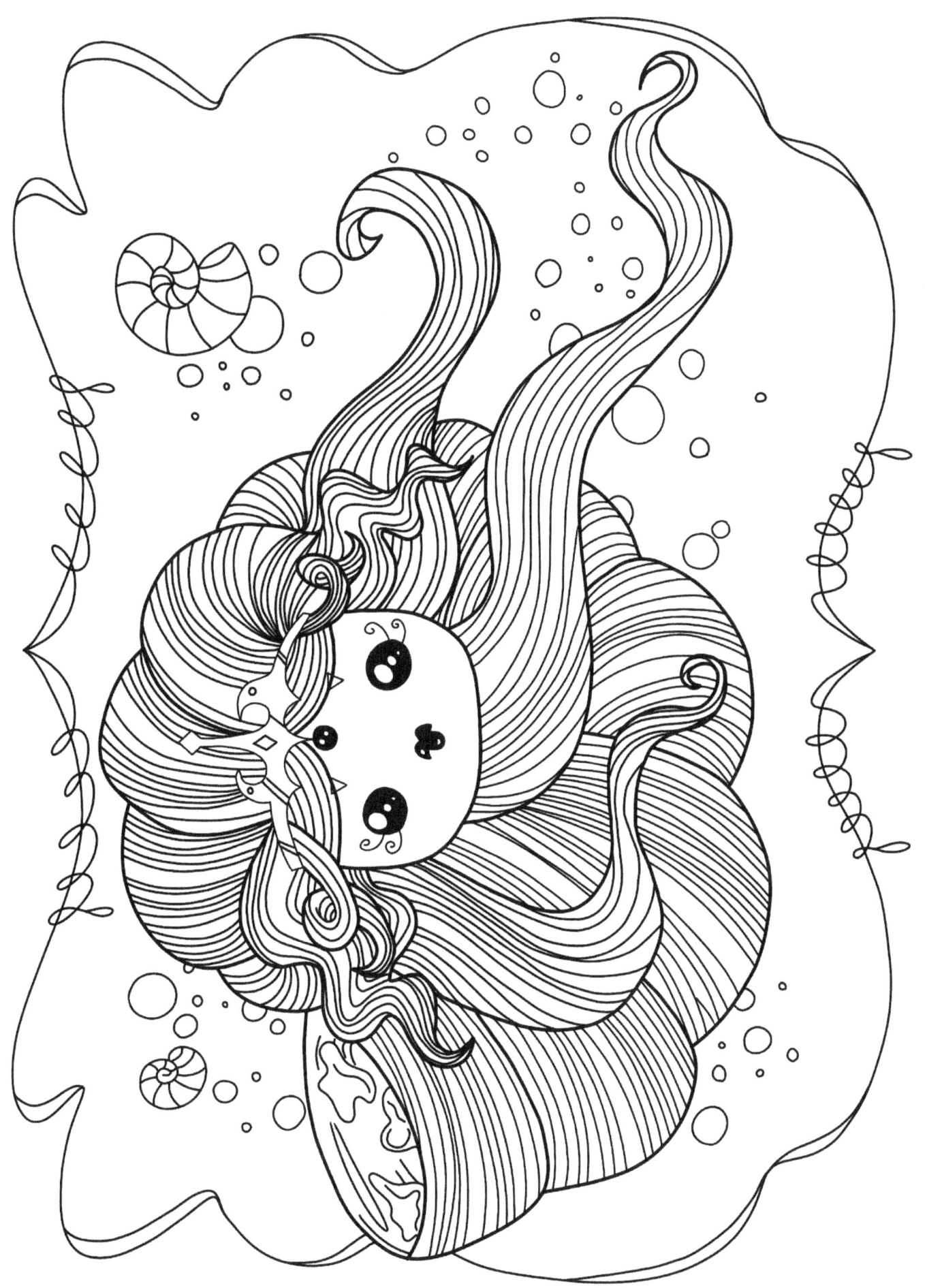

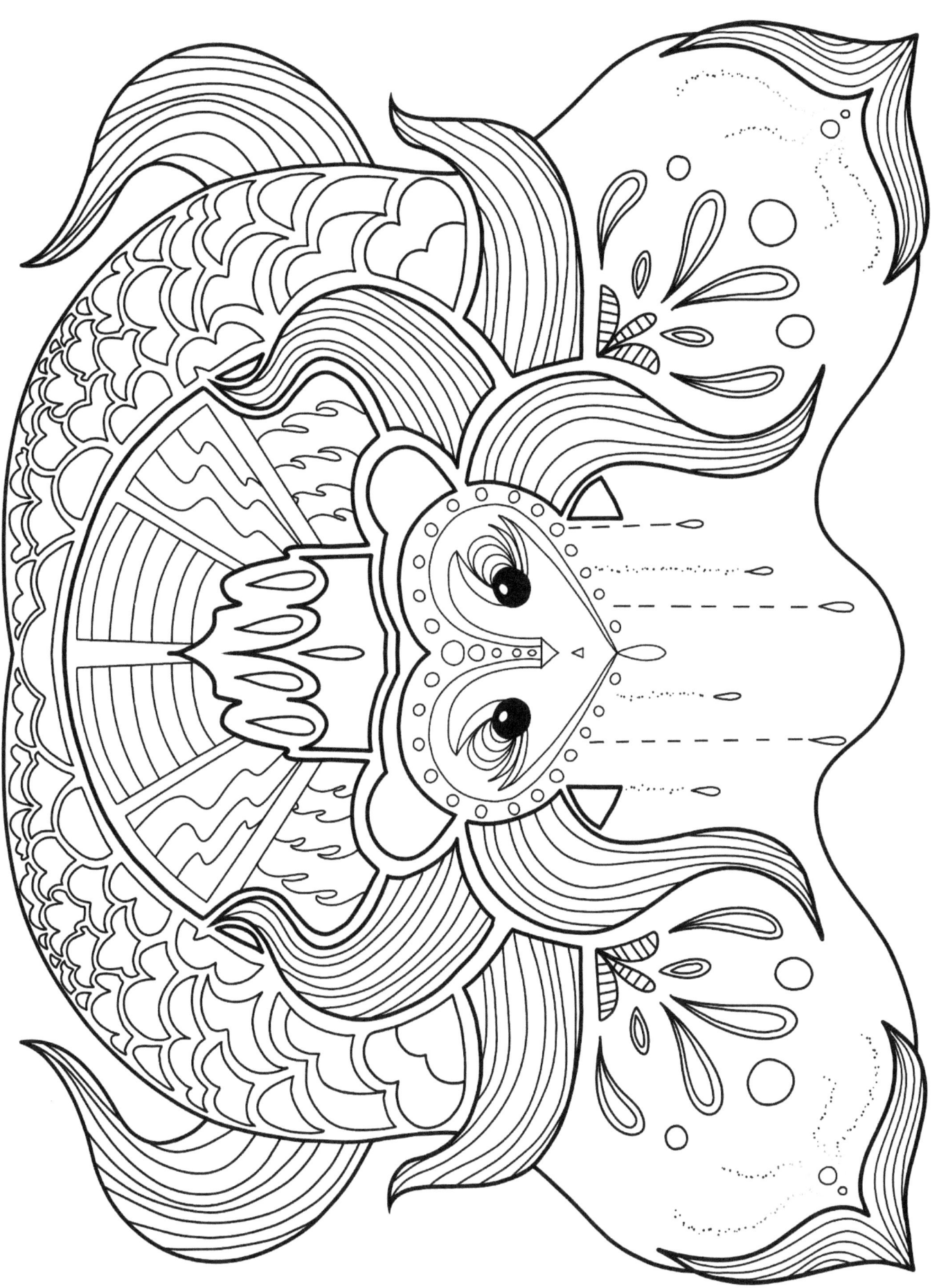

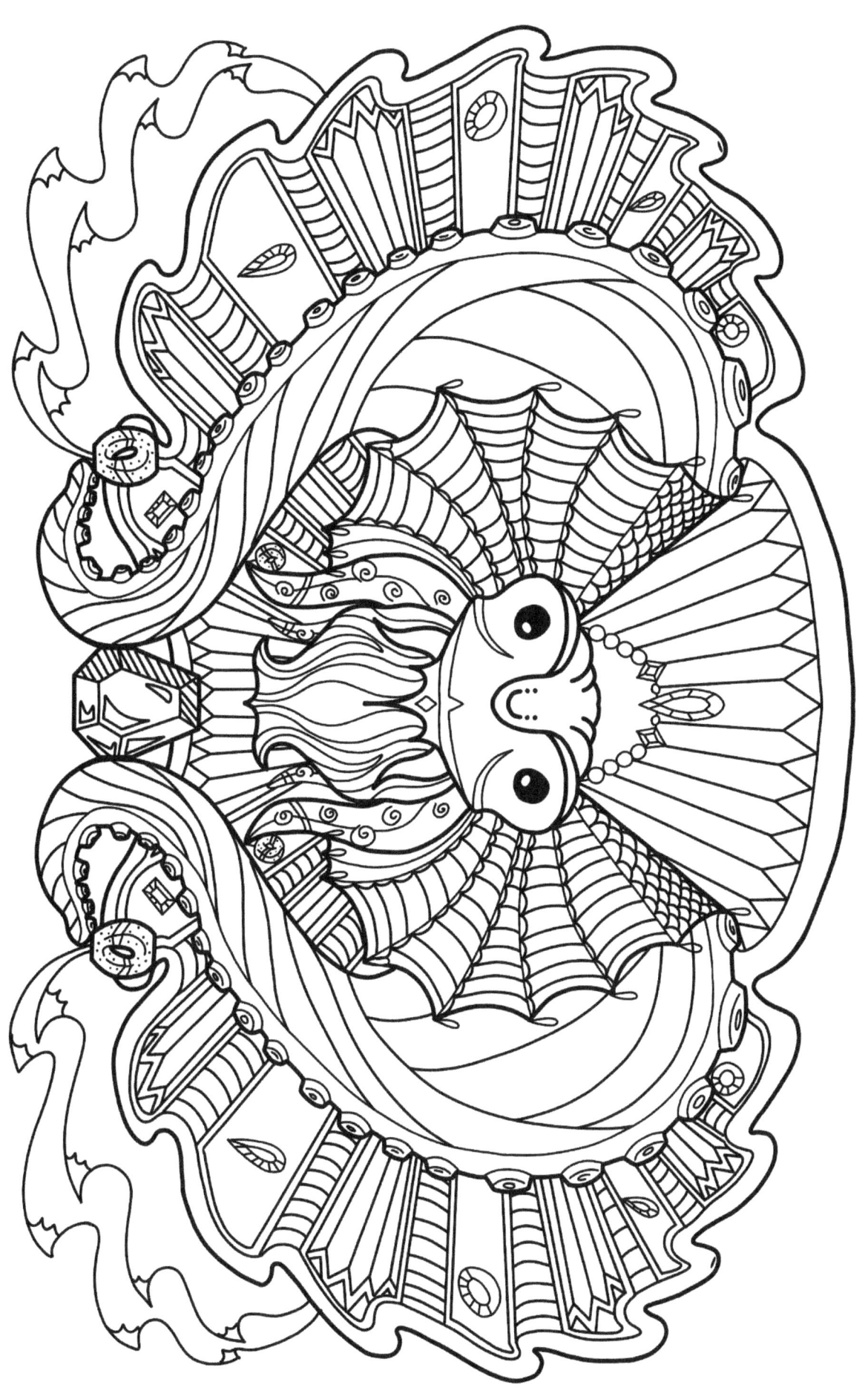

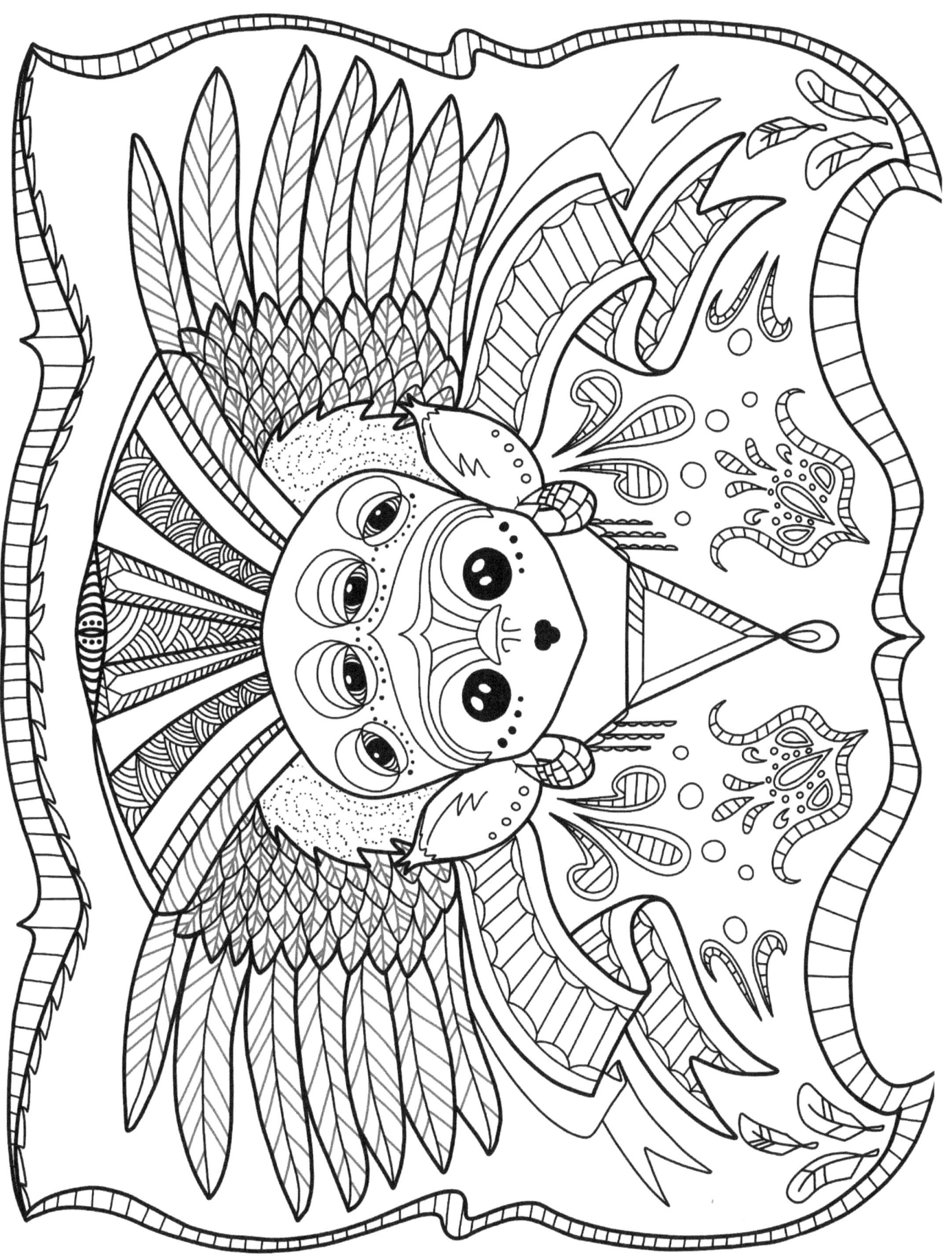

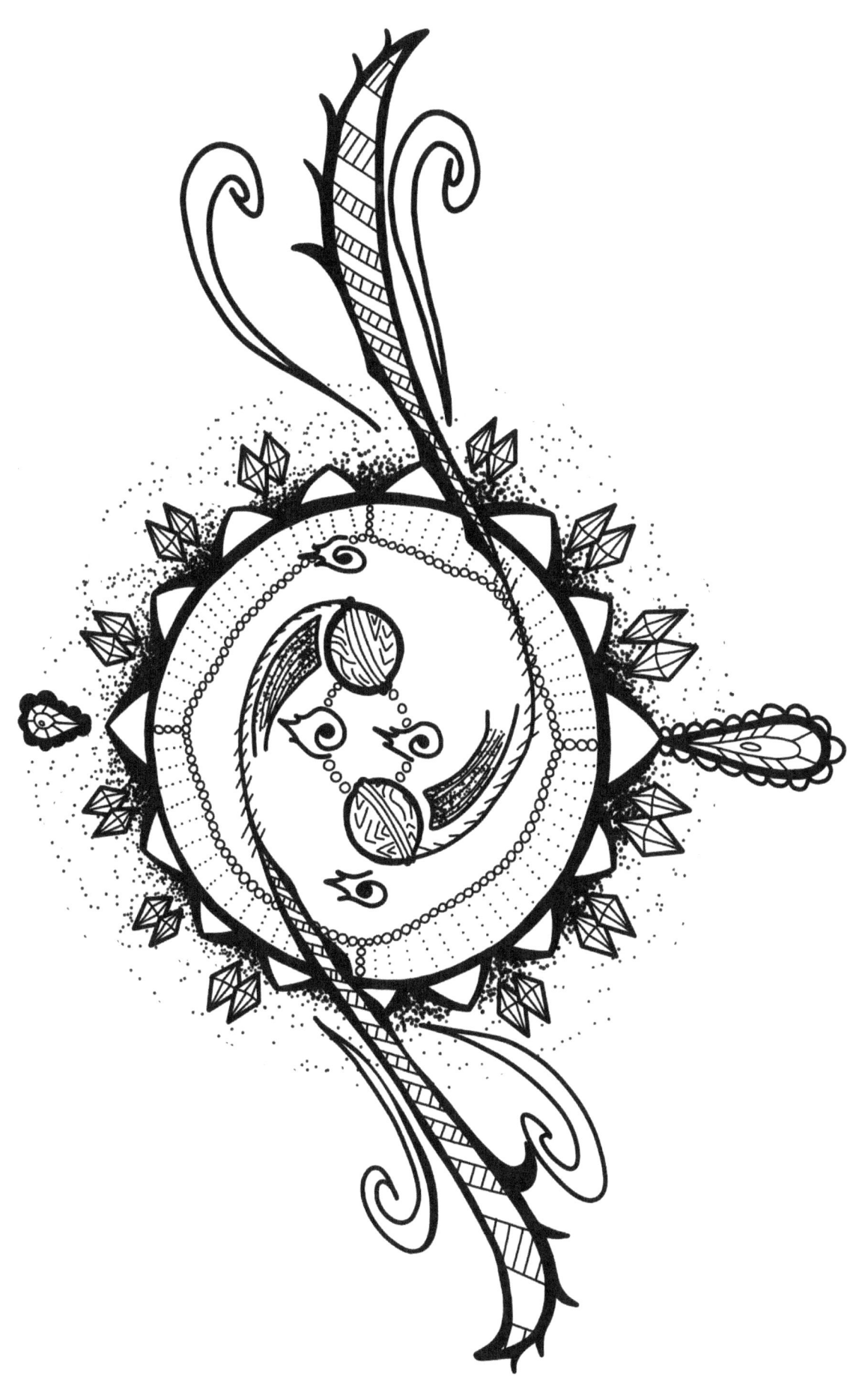

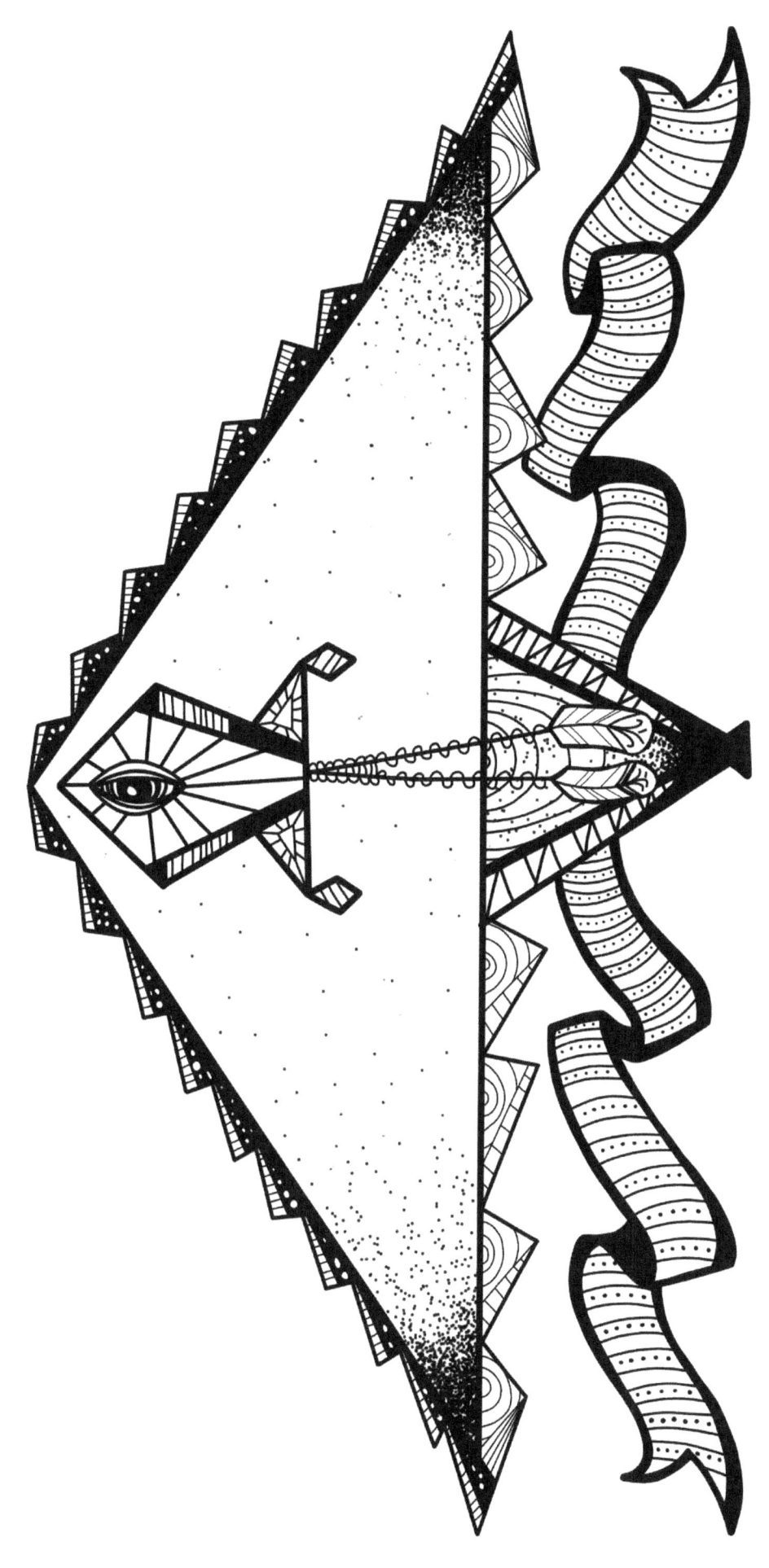

www.ingramcontent.com/pod-product-compliance
Lightning Source LLC
Chambersburg PA
CBHW062345220526
45469CB00008B/2839